HOW TO GET HELP

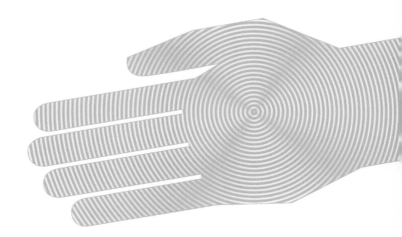

Junior Drug Awareness

Alcohol

Amphetamines and Other Uppers

Crack and Cocaine

Ecstasy and Other Designer Drugs

Heroin

How to Get Help

How to Say No

Inhalants and Solvents

LSD, PCP, and Other Hallucinogens

Marijuana

Nicotine and Cigarettes

Pain Relievers, Diet Pills, and
   Other Over-the-Counter Drugs

Prozac and Other Antidepressants

Steroids

Valium and Other Downers

Junior Drug Awareness

HOW TO GET HELP

Introduction by **BARRY R. McCAFFREY**
Director, Office of National Drug Control Policy

Foreword by **STEVEN L. JAFFE, M.D.**
Senior Consulting Editor,
Professor of Child and Adolescent Psychiatry, Emory University

Richard Kozar

Chelsea House Publishers
Philadelphia

To my daughter, Macy, who read aloud the final draft of this book and helped me see it through the eyes of a 10-year-old. —R. K.

CHELSEA HOUSE PUBLISHERS
Editor in Chief Stephen Reginald
Production Manager Pamela Loos
Director of Photography Judy L. Hasday
Art Director Sara Davis
Managing Editor James D. Gallagher
Senior Production Editor LeeAnne Gelletly

Staff for HOW TO GET HELP
Senior Editor Therese De Angelis
Associate Art Director Takeshi Takahashi
Designer Keith Trego
Picture Researcher Patricia Burns
Cover Illustrator/Designer Keith Trego

Cover photo PhotoDisc, Vol. 24 #24158

The Chelsea House World Wide Website address is http://www.chelseahouse.com

First Printing
1 3 5 7 9 8 6 4 2

Library of Congress Cataloging-in-Publication Data
Kozar, Richard.
How to get help / Richard Kozar.
   p.   cm. — (Junior drug awareness)
Includes bibliographical references and index.
Summary: Discusses the nature of drugs, both good and bad, the different kinds of drugs and their effects, why people use them, how to tell when someone has a drug problem, and how to get help.
ISBN 0-7910-5180-3
1. Drug abuse—United States–Juvenile literature. 2. Drug abuse—United States—Prevention—Juvenile literature. [1. Drugs. 2. Drug abuse.] I. Title. II. Series.
HV5809.5.K69 1999
362.29'18—dc21   99-31425
                                                            CIP

CONTENTS

by Barry R. McCaffrey
Director, Office of National
Drug Control Policy

STAYING AWAY FROM ILLEGAL DRUGS, TOBACCO PRODUCTS, AND ALCOHOL

Good health allows you to be as strong, happy, smart, and skillful as you can possibly be. The worst thing about illegal drugs is that they damage people from the inside. Our bodies and minds are wonderful, complicated systems that run like finely tuned machines when we take care of ourselves.

Doctors prescribe legal drugs, called medicines, to heal us when we become sick, but dangerous chemicals that are not recommended by doctors, nurses, or pharmacists are called illegal drugs. These drugs cannot be bought in stores because they harm different organs of the body, causing illness or even death. Illegal drugs, such as marijuana, cocaine or "crack," heroin, methamphetamine ("meth"), and other dangerous substances are against the law because they affect our ability to think, work, play, sleep, or eat.

If anyone ever offers you illegal drugs or any kind of pills, liquids, substances to smoke, or shots to inject into your body, tell them you're not interested. You should report drug pushers —people who distribute these poisons—to parents, teachers, police, coaches, clergy, or other adults whom you trust.

Cigarettes and alcohol are also illegal for youngsters. Tobacco products and drinks like wine, beer, and liquor are particularly harmful for children and teenagers because their bodies, especially their nervous systems, are still developing. For this reason, young people are more likely to be hurt by illicit drugs—including cigarettes and alcohol. These two products kill more people—from cancer, and automobile accidents caused by intoxicated drivers—than all other drugs combined. We say about drug use: "Users are losers." Be a winner and stay away from illegal drugs, tobacco products, and alcoholic beverages.

Here are four reasons why you shouldn't use illegal drugs:

- Illegal drugs can cause brain damage.
- Illegal drugs are "psychoactive." This means that they change your personality or the way you feel. They also impair your judgment. While under the influence of drugs, you are more likely to endanger your life or someone else's. You will also be less able to protect yourself from danger.
- Many illegal drugs are addictive, which means that once a person starts taking them, stopping is extremely difficult. An addict's body craves the drug and becomes dependent upon it. The illegal drug–user may become sick if the drug is discontinued and so may become a slave to drugs.

- Some drugs, called "gateway" substances, can lead a person to take more-dangerous drugs. For example, a 12-year-old who smokes marijuana is 79 times more likely to have an addiction problem later in life than a child who never tries marijuana.

Here are some reasons why you shouldn't drink alcoholic beverages, including beer and wine coolers:

- Alcohol is the second leading cause of death in our country. More than 100,000 people die every year because of drinking.
- Adolescents are twice as likely as adults to be involved in fatal alcohol-related car crashes.
- Half of all assaults against girls or women involve alcohol.
- Drinking is illegal if you are under the age of 21. You could be arrested for this crime.

Here are three reasons why you shouldn't smoke cigarettes:

- Nicotine is highly addictive. Once you start smoking, it is very hard to stop, and smoking cigarettes causes lung cancer and other diseases. Tobacco- and nicotine-related diseases kill more than 400,000 people every year.
- Each day, 3,000 kids begin smoking. One-third of these youngsters will probably have their lives shortened because of tobacco use.
- Children who smoke cigarettes are almost six times more likely to use other illegal drugs than kids who don't smoke.

If your parents haven't told you how they feel about the dangers of illegal drugs, ask them. One of every 10 kids aged 12 to 17 is using illegal drugs. They do not understand the risks they are taking with their health and their lives. However, the vast majority of young people in America are smart enough to figure out that drugs, cigarettes, and alcohol could rob them of their future. Be your body's best friend: guard your mental and physical health by staying away from drugs.

WHY SHOULD I LEARN ABOUT DRUGS?

Steven L. Jaffe, M.D., Senior Consulting Editor,
Professor of Child and Adolescent Psychiatry,
Emory University

Your grandparents and great-grandparents did not think much about "drug awareness." That's because drugs, to most of them, simply meant "medicine."

Of the three types of drugs, medicine is the good type. Medicines such as penicillin and aspirin promote healing and help sick people get better.

Another type of drug is obviously bad for you because it is poison. Then there are the kinds of drugs that fool you, such as marijuana and LSD. They make you feel good, but they harm your body and brain.

Our great crisis today is that this third category of drugs has become widely abused. Drugs of abuse are everywhere, not just in rough neighborhoods. Many teens are introduced to drugs by older brothers, sisters, friends, or even friends' parents. Some people may use only a little bit of a drug, but others who inherited a tendency to become addicted may move on to using drugs all the time. If a family member is or was an alcoholic or an addict, a young person is at greater risk of becoming one.

Drug abuse can weaken us physically. Worse, it can cause permanent mental damage. Our brain is the most important part of our body. Our thoughts, hopes, wishes, feelings, and memories are located there, within 100 billion nerve cells. Alcohol and drugs that are abused will harm—and even destroy—these cells. During the teen years, your brain continues to develop and grow, but drugs and alcohol can impair this growth.

I treat all types of teenagers at my hospital programs and in my office. Many suffer from depression or anxiety. A lot of them abuse drugs and alcohol, and this makes their depression or fears worse. I have celebrated birthdays and high school graduations with many of my patients. But I have also been to sad funerals for others who have died from problems with drug abuse.

Doctors understand more about drugs today than ever before. We've learned that some substances (even some foods) that we once thought were harmless can actually cause health problems. And for some people, medicines that help relieve one symptom might cause problems in other ways. This is because each person's body chemistry and immune system are different.

For all of these reasons, drug awareness is important for everyone. We need to learn which drugs to avoid or question—not only the destructive, illegal drugs we hear so much about in the news, but also ordinary medicines we buy at the supermarket or pharmacy. We need to understand that even "good" drugs can hurt us if they are not used correctly. We also need accurate scientific knowledge, not just rumors we hear from other teens.

Drug awareness enables you to make good decisions. It allows you to become powerful and strong and have a meaningful life!

Despite what you may think, alcohol is a drug. In fact, it is one of the most widely abused drugs in the United States. And alcoholics —people who are addicted to alcohol—are not the only people with drinking problems. One 1997 survey estimated that about 11.2 million Americans are "heavy drinkers," meaning they consume five or more drinks on the same occasion more than five times a month.

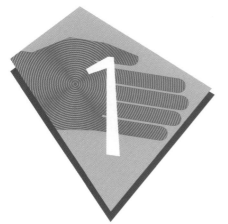

ARE ALL DRUGS BAD?

When most young people hear the word "drugs," the first thought that comes to mind may be that all drugs are bad. After all, everywhere kids look, it seems, there are reminders to stay away from drugs and warnings about what drugs can do to your mind and your health.

But the truth is, some drugs are very good for us. In fact, many people would not be able to survive without certain drugs, such as penicillin (the name given to a group of drugs that fight bacterial infections) or bronchodilators (drugs that help people suffering from asthma to breathe more easily). Drugs that are dangerous, however, both for kids and adults, are illegal drugs and those taken not to cure an ailment or relieve pain but for the temporary "high," or good feeling, they create.

You may be surprised to learn that the **nicotine**

found in tobacco products and the alcohol found in beer, wine, and other types of liquor are also drugs. Although it is legal for adults to drink alcohol and use tobacco, doing so is not necessarily safe, especially when these drugs are used excessively.

When a person can't stop smoking, drinking alcohol, or taking another drug, he or she has become **physically dependent** on the drug. This means that the person's brain has adapted to require regular doses of the drug and cannot function normally without it. In certain people who are **predisposed** to become physically dependant on drugs, **addiction** may result. A person who is addicted to a drug continues to take it despite severe negative consequences. When a person who is physically dependent or addicted stops taking the drug, he or she experiences unpleasant physical symptoms. This is known as **withdrawal**, and depending on the drug that has been abused, it can be life-threatening.

Not only the body but also the mind can become "hooked" on drugs. For example, people who abuse **marijuana** can develop **psychological dependence**, meaning that even if they stop using the drug and have no physical urge to take it, they still feel compelled to use the drug.

Becoming addicted to any drug, physically or mentally, is dangerous for several reasons. For starters, those who become addicted to "hard" drugs, such as **cocaine** or **heroin**, have a difficult time caring about anyone but themselves and the drug they're addicted to. Even when bad things happen as a result of their drug use, they can-

Do you smoke? Do you think you can quit after trying "just a few" cigarettes? You may be dead wrong. Studies show that an addiction to nicotine is stronger in those who begin smoking at a young age than in those who start as adults. And more than 90 percent of adult smokers started when they were teens. They didn't think they'd get addicted to nicotine either.

not seem to stop using. Second, people who abuse drugs are endangering their lives. Dozens of teens and young adults who abuse alcohol die every year from just one night of heavy drinking because their bodies can't tolerate a great amount of alcohol in a brief period.

Furthermore, years of drinking alcohol or using other drugs damage the brain, lungs, liver, kidneys, and other important organs. Drug use affects one's ability to think, reason, learn, remember, and solve problems. And finally, many of the drugs people become dependent on, such as marijuana, cocaine, and heroin, are illegal in this country. This means that anyone caught using, selling, or possessing them can be arrested and imprisoned.

Gateway Drugs

Tobacco, alcohol, and marijuana are typically the first drugs kids experiment with. This is why they are sometimes called **gateway drugs**—they often open the "gateway" or make it easier to abuse other drugs. Despite the popular myth that alcohol, cigarettes, and pot are fairly harmless, gateway drugs can be dangerous and addictive themselves. Studies show that if you never try gateway drugs, it is highly unlikely that you will ever abuse any drugs.

Alcohol kills more people than all other drugs combined, except nicotine. Because drinking alcohol is common in American society, it's not surprising that it is the most abused drug in the country and one of the first drugs teens try. And make no mistake: *alcohol is a drug*. It alters your mind, the way your body functions, and your overall health. Alcohol affects the brain's ability to relay messages to the rest of the body. It affects coordination, timing, and judgment. This is why it is dangerous for people to drive or operate other machinery after they've had alcohol. In 1997, 16,189 people in the United States were killed in car crashes involving alcohol. That's an average of one death every 32 minutes. That same year, more than *1 million* people—an average of one every 30 seconds—were injured in alcohol-related car crashes.

The physical effects of excessive alcohol use are especially harmful to children and teens, whose bodies are still developing. And drinking "just a beer" or "just a wine cooler" is no less harmful: a 12-ounce can of beer, a $4^1/_2$-ounce glass of wine, and one ounce of hard liquor all contain the same amount of alcohol. So despite what you may hear, drinking "a couple of beers" is *still* drinking.

In 1991, 10.5 million children in grades 7 through 12 consumed more than 1 billion cans of beer. Kids ages 12 to 18 consume 35 percent of all the wine coolers sold in the United States. By the time they are high school seniors, 35 percent have engaged in **binge drinking** (drinking excessive amounts at one time) in the past month.

While adults who drink small amounts of alcohol can temporarily feel relaxed or happy, not everyone knows when to stop drinking. Some people may find themselves drinking regularly, maybe even daily, and not always when they are with others. Some who drink heavily also become alcoholics, meaning that they cannot control their urge to drink.

We now know that alcoholism is a disease, and that it affects more than 5 million Americans, including teens. Even so, many teens who have been surveyed say they have already had their first taste of alcohol. Underage drinking can cause more problems than just getting you in trouble at home or school. It can have many serious consequences. The younger a person is when he or she first begins drinking, the greater the chance of developing a drinking problem. Youngsters who begin drinking before they are 15 are twice as likely to abuse the drug and four times more likely to become alcoholics than those who wait until they are 21 to try alcohol.

In addition, underage drinkers are more likely to practice unsafe sex or drive while intoxicated—which greatly increases the odds of being in an automobile accident. More than one-third of the young adults ages 15 to 20 who died in auto accidents in 1996 had been involved with alcohol.

The cigarette and tobacco habit is second only to alcohol in popularity among teenagers. Nicotine, which is found in all tobacco products, including cigarettes, cigars, chewing tobacco, and snuff, stimulates the nervous system in the same way that cocaine does, and it can be just as addictive.

Nicotine is a **stimulant**, a drug that increases the body's activities, such as heart rate and blood pressure. It can also worsen or cause bronchitis, asthma, impaired breathing, and eventually even deadly ailments such as cancer, lung diseases, and heart disease.

Every year, more than 400,000 Americans die prematurely from diseases caused by cigarette smoking. This is greater than the number of deaths from AIDS, alcohol, car accidents, murders, suicides, fires, and other drugs combined. Yet most teens believe that smoking for a couple of years will not harm them, and very few think they will actually become lifelong cigarette addicts. Four and one-half million American kids ages 18 and younger now smoke—that's nearly one out of five. Another

3,000 youngsters take up smoking every day.

But as any smoker can tell you, "kicking the habit" is very difficult. The withdrawal symptoms from quitting nicotine can be painful and bothersome: within hours of quitting, a smoker's heartbeat slows, and he or she feels cranky or sick. A strong craving for the drug can last for weeks, months, or even years after the former smoker stops using the drug. And as a gateway drug, nicotine frequently leads to use of even more-dangerous drugs. The National Center on Addiction and Substance Abuse at Columbia University reports that a 12- to 17-year-old who smokes cigarettes is 19 times more likely to use cocaine than one who does not smoke.

A third gateway drug is marijuana, which is derived from the hemp plant (its scientific name is *Cannabis sativa*). This plant has been used for centuries to make rope, fabric, and paper. But when ingested, either by eating the leaves or inhaling the smoke from burning leaves, the plant becomes a drug.

Lots of people know how marijuana makes you feel, but did you know that the cannabis plant contains more than 400 chemicals? Several of them are **psychoactive**, which means that they can alter or change your brain. The chemical with the strongest effect on the brain is THC (delta-9 tetrahydrocannabinol), which is found in the resin of the plant. THC levels are the highest in the flower of the cannabis plant, which holds the highest concentration of resin.

Marijuana available on the street today is much stronger than it was 30 years ago. In the 1960s and

Smoking marijuana may seem harmless, but it can mess up your life. Your performance in school, sports, and other activities will suffer if you're high. And someone who smokes five joints per week inhales as many cancer-causing chemicals as someone who smokes 20 cigarettes—a full pack—during the same period. Marijuana users may also develop many of the same respiratory problems that tobacco smokers have, including chronic bronchitis and inflamed sinuses.

1970s, the level of THC in cannabis plants was usually between 0.25 and 1 percent. Marijuana harvested in the United States today has THC levels that frequently exceed 20 percent. This increased potency not only makes marijuana more intoxicating but also increases the health risks to those who use it. In addition, the feeling of euphoria that users may feel can also become frightening. Marijuana users may experience **paranoia**—they may begin feeling that others are watching them or are out to get them.

Today's marijuana users are starting to use the drug at an increasingly younger age. In 1997, half of all high school seniors surveyed said that they had tried marijuana at least once. And a recent report from a yearly government study on drug use called "Monitoring the Future" showed that the average age when kids first try marijuana is now $13^1/_2$ years old.

The THC in marijuana interferes with coordination, balance, and sense of time. It also increases the body's blood pressure level and heart rate. The popular myth that marijuana is safer than most other illegal drugs is not true: there are actually *more* carcinogenic (cancer-causing) chemicals in marijuana smoke than in cigarette smoke. Long-term use of "pot" can damage your immune system, which fights off diseases and illness. And THC is not eliminated from the body immediately; it remains for days or even weeks after marijuana is actually smoked or eaten.

Although research shows that marijuana is not addictive, people who use the drug can become psychologically dependent on it. Marijuana also impairs short-term memory and the ability to concentrate. One 16-year-old boy who used to smoke pot described its effects this way: "Marijuana makes you stupid."

Cocaine and Crack

Also known as "coke," "nose candy," and "snow," cocaine reached its peak of popularity during the 1980s, when it seemed to be in the news constantly, along with the daredevil crowd who used it. And the news was all bad.

Comedian John Belushi, who was a regular for years

on the popular late-night TV show *Saturday Night Live*, died in 1982 from an overdose of cocaine mixed with heroin (a deadly combination known as a "speedball"). College basketball player Len Bias, who in 1986 was celebrating the signing of a pro basketball contract with the Boston Celtics, suffered a fatal heart attack from his first dose of cocaine. He was 22 years old.

Cocaine is a white powder made from the leaves of the coca plant, which grows primarily in the Andes Mountains of South America. Like other strong stimulants, such as **amphetamines**, the drug increases heart rate, blood pressure, and body temperature. It dilates the pupils of the eyes and causes blood vessels to constrict (tighten). People who take cocaine regularly will lose their appetite and have difficulty sleeping while they are on the drug. They may feel restless, anxious, and irritable.

It is not unusual for a cocaine user to take an **overdose** (enough of the drug to produce seizures or cause death). Overdoses can also lead to strokes, cerebral hemorrhages (heavy bleeding in the brain), and heart attacks. And there is no medicine that can stop the effects of a cocaine overdose. Heavy users of cocaine quickly develop a **tolerance** for the drug, which means that their bodies have adapted to require more of the drug to produce the same results they once felt with smaller doses.

Cocaine is usually inhaled through the nose (called "snorting"), but some users also melt and inject the drug into their bodies using a hypodermic needle. It takes only

Cocaine, shown here in small vials, is the strongest stimulant found naturally; using the drug even once can cause a heart attack, stroke, or even death. An even deadlier form of the drug is crack: by 1988, crack was responsible for more drug-related overdoses and deaths in the United States than any other illegal drug.

seconds for the drug to produce a powerful high, but within an hour, that high wears off and the user feels an intense craving for the drug. Using cocaine just once can cause addiction—and as we have seen, just one try can also kill.

Another form of cocaine—and a much cheaper one—is called **crack**, or rock cocaine. It's made by mixing cocaine powder with baking soda and then heating it. The final, cooled product resembles rocks, and makes a crackling sound when it is smoked.

Crack makes users feel high very quickly, within 10 to 20 seconds of being smoked, but the excited feeling seldom lasts longer than 10 or 20 minutes. Then, users just as quickly "crash," or quickly begin to feel terrible. Crack addicts end up buying huge quantities of the drug to maintain highs that are shorter and less intense each time.

Crack is 10 times more addictive than regular cocaine, according to studies. Addicts have been known to go without eating or sleeping for hours or days at a time to avoid coming down from their highs. They've also been known to steal money or commit other crimes to pay for their drug addiction.

Babies born to mothers who use the drug come into the world addicted themselves, and are known as "crack babies." Hundreds of thousands of these unlucky infants are born each year in the United States, and they need extensive medical treatment to recover from the addiction passed on to them by their mothers.

Heroin

Along with cocaine and crack, heroin is one of the most addictive and dangerous drugs available. And yet, like cocaine, it comes from a harmless-looking plant called *Papaver somniferum*, or "sleep-inducing poppy." Cultivators of heroin slice open the base of the poppy flower and collect the milky sap that oozes out. This sap eventually darkens and congeals into a brown substance called **opium**.

Like many chemicals that come from plants, opium has beneficial medical uses. For example, scientists learned in the early part of the 20th century that

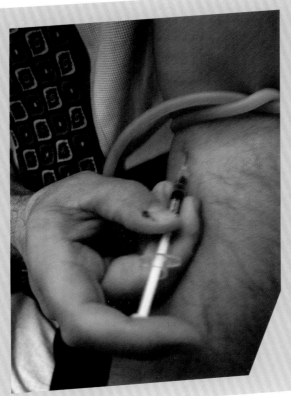

A heroin user injects the drug into his arm through a vein. The user has tightened a band around his arm so that the vein swells and is easy to find with the needle. Injecting heroin is not the only way to become addicted to the drug, but it does carry additional dangers, such as damaged or infected veins, possible death from an air bubble entering the bloodstream, and the risk of becoming infected with HIV, the virus that causes AIDS.

painkilling drugs made from opium, such as morphine and codeine (which is found in some prescription cough syrups), can help people with certain health problems.

Heroin, on the other hand, has no medical use and is extremely dangerous. One of the reasons for this is that it is made illegally and therefore its purity and strength are not regulated the way prescription drugs are.

In past years, heroin sold illegally in the United States was usually heavily diluted, or "cut," by drug dealers who wanted to make more money and have their drug supply last longer. Most street heroin before 1990 was rarely even 10 percent pure. Beginning in the 1990s,

All of the common household and school products shown here—felt-tip markers, nail polish remover, rubber cement, and nail polish—are considered inhalants. They can be deadly when used to get high.

however, more of the drug became available, and the purity rose sharply, to 50 or 60 percent. This very strong heroin is often smoked or snorted like cocaine, rather than taken through the more common method of injection. Injecting heroin into the veins, or "mainlining," is especially dangerous because when hypodermic needles are shared, the risk of contracting AIDS becomes extremely high.

Unfortunately, many young people mistakenly believe that smoking or snorting heroin is safer and less addictive than injecting. They're wrong on both counts. According to recent surveys from the early 1990s to the mid-1990s, the number of eighth and tenth graders using heroin doubled. And most users who start off snorting or smoking the drug end up injecting it once they become addicted.

Chronic use of heroin causes serious physical and mental problems, including frequent infections, severe depression and suicidal thoughts, inflammation of the lungs, liver, kidneys, or brain, and diseases such as AIDS or tetanus. Overdosing is common and quite easy to do.

Inhalants

Inhalants are substances whose fumes are inhaled to produce intoxication. This kind of drug is often used by kids who begin experimenting with dangerous substances while still very young. This is because most of these substances are common household or commercial products that are readily available in homes, groceries, drugstores, and home improvement shops. The most common inhalants kids "sniff" (inhale by the nose) or "huff" (inhale by the mouth) are **solvents** such as airplane glue, paint thinner, butane (from cigarette lighters), furniture polish, nail polish, gasoline, correction fluid, and felt-tip markers. Other products used as inhalants are **aerosols** like hair spray and spray paint, or gases, like Freon, found in refrigerants for car and home use. The fumes of inhalants are breathed directly into the lungs from the original container, from a plastic or paper bag (this is called "bagging"), or from an inhalant-soaked rag.

Because inhalants are easy to come by and are not illegal when used according to package directions, many teenagers have tried them at least once. The youngest teens are the biggest abusers. The Monitoring the Future study reported in 1996 that more than one in five eighth graders (22 percent) have used inhalants at some point in their lives.

Inhalants produce a quick and brief high, which is followed by drowsiness, dizziness, and often confusion. Although they may seem less harmful than illegal drugs, these products—even when they are used properly—are toxic (poisonous) chemicals that can cause brain damage or kill, even with the first use. And it is extremely difficult to control how much of these substances one is inhaling. Just one try can cause "sudden sniffing death," a condition in which an abuser's heart becomes over-stimulated and the person dies almost immediately.

Other Dangerous Drugs

The Office of National Drug Control Policy (ONDCP) in Washington, D.C., regularly publishes reports tracking how illegal drugs are used and distributed in the United States. The 1997 ONDCP report listed the following drugs as "emerging," or becoming popular across the country:

- **Methamphetamine**—an extremely dangerous and addictive stimulant, also known as "meth," "crank," or "ice," that is smoked, snorted, or injected. Side effects include confusion, paranoia, aggressive and violent behavior, heart failure, and brain damage.
- "Club drugs"—the nickname given to a variety of drugs used at nightclubs and "raves" (large parties

open to the public and held in locations like warehouses, basements, and unused buildings). The most popular club drugs are usually **hallucinogens** such as **Ecstasy** (see below).

- Hallucinogens—one of the most popular hallucinogens (drugs that distort the user's perception of events or cause them to perceive objects or visions that are not real) is **LSD.** LSD is sold in tablets, capsules, or liquid; the liquid is sometimes soaked into small squares of blotter paper. "Acid," as it is called, causes hallucinations and creates an altered state of time and self. The drug's effects are unpredictable; a "bad trip" can cause intense panic and terror. Another hallucinogen is MDMA, best known as Ecstasy. MDMA is one of a group of substances called "designer drugs." The chemical structures of these drugs closely resemble those of some prescription or illegal drugs.

Now that you've read about what certain drugs can do to you, you may be wondering why anyone would begin using them in the first place. In the next chapter, we'll look at some of the reasons people turn to addictive or dangerous drugs.

Why do people use drugs? Some kids say they turn to drugs to ease feelings of loneliness, to fit in with their friends, or to have fun. But do these sound like good reasons to risk your health and your life?

WHY DO SOME PEOPLE USE DRUGS?

f you are a happy, confident person, you may have a hard time understanding why kids or grown-ups would even think of abusing nicotine, alcohol, or other drugs. But it's important to remember that drug problems affect people all over the world, people of all ages, races, and beliefs. No one is immune.

Every one of us is occasionally tempted to do things we shouldn't—including abusing drugs—even though we know that doing so is bad for us. The trouble with drug use is that although teens, and even adults, may want to try an addictive substance just once, just to "see what it's like," that one occasion may be all it takes to become addicted, especially with drugs like cocaine and heroin.

Drugs have ruined the lives of rich kids as well as poor ones, honor students and average ones, popular kids and loners. While some drug abusers may come

Some people use drugs to escape stress or frustration. Others use them to relieve pain or anger. In reality, drug abuse does not solve problems. In fact, it usually creates even greater ones.

from tough neighborhoods where violence is common and their families are under constant strain, others may live in the finest neighborhoods and have everything they could want or need.

There is no single reason why people use drugs. However, youngsters who are asked about drug use in surveys often mention some of the same reasons.

Peer Pressure

We all know what it feels like to want to belong to a social group. But what happens when someone in the group does something you don't agree with or don't want to do? What if, on the way to a concert, one of your friends pulls out a joint? Even if you don't want to smoke pot, everyone else seems to be doing it. What do you do?

The feeling you experience when you're in a situation like this is called **peer pressure**. A peer—a friend, a sibling, or someone else of your own age group—does or says something to make you feel as though you have to act like them to fit in. Sometimes, peer pressure is easy to spot. A person might come right out and say something to make you feel bad. "Come on, don't be a baby," your friend might say, or "Everyone else is doing it." Even if your friends don't say anything specific, you may still worry that they won't like you if you don't go along with them.

Peer pressure is one of the main reasons why kids begin using drugs. Adults feel peer pressure too, but when you're growing up and trying to figure out exactly where you fit in, the feeling can be much stronger. That's why even if you don't want to try drugs, you might be tempted to take a drink of alcohol or puff on a cigarette.

Stress

Pressure from friends or relatives isn't the only reason kids start using drugs. Sometimes the stress that people feel when they are in difficult situations may also lead them to try drugs. People who have already tried drugs may have discovered that these substances can make them feel better for a short time. But in the long run, drugs won't solve anyone's troubles or make life more exciting. Many times, drugs make problems worse,

What Makes You Feel Better About Yourself?

I n May 1998, *USA Weekend Magazine* conducted a survey of more than 250,000 students in grades 6 through 12 to find out what they thought of themselves and what most influenced their self-image. The survey asked kids what they liked most and least about themselves. Half of the students said they felt "really good" about themselves, and half said they did not. The chart on the right shows the percentage of teens who chose ways they thought they could improve themselves and enhance their self-image.

and they make users seem less responsible and mature. Often, drug use even creates new problems.

It's perfectly normal to feel some stress. In fact, a certain level of stress may help you perform better. For example, say you're about to join your teammates in a soccer game, and you feel nervous. That nervousness may help you, because it makes you feel more alert. However, when some people are under an enormous amount of stress and feel overpowered by it, they may turn to drugs for a temporary way to forget their problems.

Question:	Which of the following would make you feel better about yourself?*	
	Getting better grades	49%
	Bulking/toning up	38%
	Losing weight	38%
	Doing better at sports	36%
	Having a better relationship with parents	30%
	Wearing better clothes	24%
	Fitting in with a certain crowd	16%
	Nothing; I like myself the way I am	15%
	Quitting smoking	8%

(*Teens responded to more than one choice in survey)

None of the students mentioned using drugs as a way to improve themselves. Using drugs will *not* help you to look better, feel better, or lead a more interesting life. But you can choose other ways to do so.

Source: *USA Weekend Magazine*, May 1, 1998

Low Self-Worth

Some people use drugs because they don't feel good about themselves or have faith in what they can accomplish. This is known as having low self-worth. Kids who suffer from this problem may think that they are not as "good" as their friends or schoolmates because they don't dress as well, they aren't as good-looking, athletic, smart, or funny, or they don't have interesting things to say. Sometimes, when people feel that they're not wor-

Do you smoke cigarettes because most of your friends do? Do you drink beer because it makes you feel "mellow"? Do you use marijuana or speed because you know your parents disapprove? Guess what? You're not alone. These reasons reflect perfectly normal emotions. Yet there are many drug-free ways to relax, fit in with your friends, or communicate with your parents. Read Chapter 5 for some ideas.

thy of love or attention, they may begin to take drugs to try to forget how bad they usually feel or to feel more "normal," more like other kids. One of the worst situations is when kids do not receive love and support at home, from their parents and family members. Children who are treated badly at home often stop taking care of themselves, and this may include turning to drugs.

But as we have seen, getting high lasts only a short time, and the risks of using drugs far outweigh the brief "rush" one may get from them. With love, attention, and professional help, kids suffering from low self-worth can learn to change how they see themselves and learn to realize that they are worthwhile and important.

Other Reasons Why Some Kids Use Drugs

Here are some of the other reasons that young people have given for using drugs:

- To have fun or relax
- To feel more grown up
- Out of curiosity
- Because it seems exciting or rebellious
- To stop feeling lonely or depressed

Nothing is wrong with having any of these emotions. Everyone feels them at one time or another. But it is important to try to find ways to satisfy these feelings in ways that are healthier than using drugs.

"Instant" Society

We can contact someone on the other side of the world instantly by using a telephone, fax machine, or Internet connection. Airplanes and even cars carry us at speeds that were unthinkable 100 years ago. Advances in science and medicine help prevent and cure numerous illnesses that were once fatal and can shorten the time needed to recover from sickness or accidents.

These improvements have made life easier and better for millions of people. But because everything seems to be moving and working so quickly, some people expect instant solutions to all of their problems.

Many important parts of life—learning, being creative, growing physically, and accomplishing great things—take time and energy. Some people become easily frustrated when their desires are not met or problems cannot be solved right away. A few decide that taking chemicals into their bodies will bring instant happiness, pleasure, or insight. Instead, they get misery, discomfort, more problems, and sometimes addiction.

Mixed Messages

Companies eager to sell their products often use words or images in their advertising to suggest that these items will provide instant gratification (reward or pleasure). If you use this toothpaste, wear this clothing, or drive this car, the ads seem to say, you will be successful, beautiful, popular, and happy.

Some of the models used to advertise products in recent years have been made to look as though they are sick from using drugs. For example, the so-called heroin chic style of modeling features pale, underweight young men and women with dark circles under their eyes, dressed in torn or scanty clothing. Seeing these models on billboards, in magazines, and on television may give some teens the idea that heroin and other drugs are glamorous or cool.

But when you think about it, this is actually a dif-

A 1996 study found that more than 11,000 American teens under 18 years old were arrested for violating DWI (driving while intoxicated) laws. Another study of 1,023 patients admitted to a hospital's shock trauma unit found that one-third had detectable levels of marijuana in their blood. A third study of 182 fatal truck accidents revealed that 16.5 percent of the drivers involved were under the influence of cocaine or other stimulants. The message is clear: using drugs while driving can kill.

ferent kind of peer pressure. Advertisers count on your seeing the models as kids like you—and wanting to buy the company's products to fit in. If celebrities and models are using drugs, the ads seem to say, why not you?

You know why. Taking drugs is foolish. It endangers your life. It can destroy your health, your family, and your grades. It is important to remember that *most kids don't take drugs of any kind.* If TV shows, movies, magazine ads, radio programs, video games, music lyrics, or Internet sites try to idealize drugs, they are doing so with hopes of selling you something. Drugs can never magically provide excitement, sex appeal, ecstasy, or enlightenment any more than the other products advertisers want you to buy.

Some celebrities also send the wrong message when it comes to drug abuse. When athletes and movie stars such as Leonardo DiCaprio smoke, for example, it seems easy to understand why so many adolescents have also begun smoking.

But other celebrities who have struggled with drug problems can set a good example if they turn their lives around. Professional golfer John Daly won several major tournaments before his career and his life began falling apart as a result of his heavy drinking. His wife divorced him, he lost a $10 million contract to promote sporting goods, and his golf game deteriorated. During one tournament, he walked off the course without a word of explanation.

But then Daly began attending a self-help group known as Alcoholics Anonymous (AA), and in the summer of 1997, he began playing pro golf again. The best sign of his comeback was when Callaway Golf, a golf-club manufacturer, agreed to sign Daly to another endorsement contract—as long as he avoids alcohol altogether and attends AA meetings each day.

"I Can Quit When I Want To"

One 15-year-old girl who smokes recently told *Newsweek*, "I've seen the commercials where they show the old lady with the hole in her throat and the smoke coming out of it. I'll never have a hole. When I'm old and 35 and want to have a baby, I'll quit. I'm young now, so my body can deal with it."

Unfortunately, she is probably mistaken: studies show that an addiction to nicotine is stronger in those who begin smoking at a young age than in those who start as adults. The news is no better when it comes to other drugs. Alcohol-addicted teens have a much tougher time kicking the habit than older users, and the disease progresses much more rapidly. An adult may become an alcoholic within 5 to 20 years, but adolescents can "hit bottom" (reach the worst phase of the disease) only six months after they begin drinking.

Studies indicate that at least 4 million teenagers in the United States are currently physically dependent or addicted to drugs. One study shows that about 1 of every 10 kids who experiment with any type of drug will probably become addicted.

What happens when someone you know develops a drug problem? How can you tell for sure? What can you say or do about it? Who do you turn to? The next two chapters will help you find answers to these questions.

If you have a drug problem, or if someone is pressuring you to try drugs, don't be afraid to seek help. Talking to a family member or other adult you trust shows that you are strong enough to help yourself.

3

WHEN A LOVED ONE HAS A DRUG PROBLEM

Most people who are having difficulties with drugs will not simply ask for help outright. In fact, drug abusers are more likely to deny the problem and try to hide the symptoms. They may be embarrassed or afraid to confide in someone close to them. Still, there are some warning signs look for if you suspect that a friend or loved one is abusing drugs. If someone you know displays one or more of the following traits, he or she may have a drug problem:

- Getting high or getting drunk on a regular basis
- Lying about the amount of alcohol or other drugs he or she uses
- Avoiding you or other friends to get high or drunk
- Giving up favorite activities or avoiding friends who don't drink alcohol or use other drugs

- Having to drink more alcohol or use increasing amounts of another drug to get the same effect
- Constantly talking about drinking alcohol or using other drugs
- Pressuring others to drink alcohol or use other drugs
- Believing that one needs alcohol or other drugs to have fun
- Getting into trouble with the law or at school for an alcohol- or other drug-related incident
- Taking risks, including sexual risks or driving under the influence of alcohol or other drugs
- Feeling run-down, hopeless, depressed, or suicidal
- Missing work or school, or performing tasks poorly because of alcohol or other drug use

Some of these signs, such as poor job or school performance and depression, might be signs of problems other than drug abuse. They could also be symptoms of an illness that you may not know about. Nevertheless, these danger signs indicate that something is wrong.

Signs of Specific Drug Abuse

Here are a few specific signs to look for if you suspect someone of abusing a particular drug:

- Nicotine—It's usually easy to tell if someone you know is using tobacco. A person who smokes will (obviously) smell like smoke. You may also see ashes or burn marks in clothing. People who use chewing tobacco usually have stains or bits of tobacco leaves on their teeth.

It's not always easy to tell whether someone you know has a drug problem. But no one is immune—even athletes and popular kids may struggle with drug dependence.

- Alcohol—Someone who has been drinking alcohol heavily may stagger, and speech may become slurred. An alcohol user's reflexes become slowed, and the person may become nauseated or even vomit. You may also be able to detect the odor of wine, beer, or liquor on the person's breath or in the air.

- Marijuana—The most obvious sign of marijuana use is redness of the eyes. The user may also act silly or giggle for no reason, seem dizzy and uncoordinated,

The best way to overcome drug dependence or addiction is to seek professional treatment. These teens are participating in a group counseling session that helps them learn how to stay drug-free.

or become extremely sleepy or hungry (a condition nicknamed "the munchies"). You may notice a sweet, burnt scent on the person's clothing or in the air. Someone who frequently uses marijuana might carry eyedrops or own drug paraphernalia such as pipes or rolling papers.

- Stimulants (cocaine, crack, and amphetamines)—Abusers of these stimulants often look sickly and begin to neglect themselves. If the abuser has been injecting the drug, you may also see needle marks on the arms or other parts of the body.

Stimulant abusers may talk constantly, speak very quickly, pace frequently, or show other forms of compulsive behavior (irrational behavior that is very difficult to control). Cocaine and amphetamine abusers can also become easily enraged or even violent. Both types of stimulants cause the pupils of the eyes to dilate and become more sensitive to light, so abusers may wear sunglasses even at night. They may perspire heavily, breathe rapidly, and experience tremors in the hands or fingers. A person who has binged on these drugs may stay awake for extremely long periods of time and then sleep for days.

Some abusers develop a mental illness called cocaine psychosis or amphetamine psychosis. A person suffering from one of these conditions feels extreme fear and paranoia. He or she may also see, hear, and feel things in a distorted way or perceive things that are not real.

- Heroin—Heroin usually causes poor coordination, slurred speech, and slow reactions. Users' pupils are very small, their eyes may be watery, and their faces may be flushed. They may vomit, especially if they are first-time users. You may notice needle marks on the user's arms, legs, or other parts of the body.
- Inhalants—These substances can cause hallucinations, numbness and tingling in the hands and feet, suffocation, or sudden death. Short-term effects of inhalant abuse include headaches, chills, tremors, and stomach cramps. Inhalant abusers may have an

unusual breath odor or a chemical smell to their clothing. They may seem disoriented, dizzy, or drunk. An inhalant abuser often has red or runny eyes or nose and has spots or sores around the mouth. You may notice signs of paint or similar products on the face, fingers, or clothing. Some inhalant abusers may carry rags (for absorbing solvents), lots of felt-tip pens, bottles of correction fluid, or other products that produce fumes. Or they may store some of these things in their school lockers or bedrooms.

Overdose

Let's suppose that the very worst result of drug abuse happens to one of your friends or family members: the person overdoses. Remember, an overdose is when someone takes more of a drug than his or her body is capable of handling. An overdose can cause a coma or death. If a person who overdoses survives, he or she may be left with a damaged heart, brain, or other organs.

People who have overdosed on alcohol or other drugs might appear to have "passed out" or fallen asleep. However, chances are you won't be able to wake them. The first thing you should do if you suspect someone has overdosed is call for professional help. Dial the familiar 911 emergency number. Give the operator your name and the address and phone number where you are. Tell the person that you're calling about someone who may have overdosed on one or more drugs.

The operator may ask you questions about the condition of the person who's overdosed and whether you

What happens if someone you know overdoses on a drug? The first thing you should do is immediately seek medical help. Depending on the drug taken, the amount and purity of the drugs, and whether other substances were also used, an overdose can lead to coma or death.

know what kinds of drugs were taken. The operator may also suggest ways you can help the person who has overdosed until medical assistance arrives.

At the hospital or emergency center, a doctor may be able to administer an antidote (a drug that reverses the harmful drug's effects). In some cases, such as with cocaine overdose, there is no known antidote. Instead, doctors try to keep the patient alive by ensuring that the important organs in the body—the heart, lungs, kidneys, and liver, for example—keep functioning until the body is able to break down the drug and eliminate it. Treatment for overdose of illegal drugs can be complicated by the fact that such drugs are not regulated and may be "cut" or diluted with other toxic substances or drugs.

How Can I Tell If I Have a Drug Problem?

What if the "someone" you know with a drug problem is *you*? If you abuse alcohol or other drugs and think that you're not like others who do, you're wrong. Just like anyone else who abuses drugs, you can seriously endanger your body and mind—and even your life. To find out whether you have a problem, try to answer the following questions honestly:

- Can I predict the next time I will use alcohol or other drugs?
- Do I feel like I need alcohol or other drugs to have fun?
- Do I turn to alcohol or other drugs to make myself feel better after an argument or confrontation?
- Do I have to use more of a drug to get the same effect I once felt with a smaller amount?
- Do I drink alcohol or use other drugs when I'm alone?
- When I drink alcohol or use other drugs, do I forget certain segments of time?
- Am I having trouble at work or school because of alcohol or other drug use?
- Do I make promises to others or to myself to stop

drinking alcohol or using other drugs, but then break them?

- Do I feel alone, scared, miserable, or depressed?

If you answered "yes" to any of the above questions, you may have a drug problem. Don't be discouraged, though. Millions of people around the world have triumphed over drug abuse and are now living healthy, drug-free lives.

Now you know how harmful some drugs can be, and you know how to look for signs of abuse. You may be wondering where to go to get help for drug abuse problems. In Chapter 4, we'll look at the many treatments available for people who want to take control of their lives and end their dependence on drugs.

This 28-year-old mother lost her job when she stole money from her employer to buy crack. During a drug treatment program for her addiction, she was not permitted to see her young son for several months. Recovering from a drug addiction is a lifelong process that requires a firm commitment, determination, and courage.

WHERE TO GO FOR HELP

What happens if you or someone you know develops a drug abuse problem? Don't despair. A broad range of support and treatment programs is available. You may even find that it's best to start seeking help in your own home or community.

Getting Help from Family and Friends

One way to get help with a drug problem is to go directly to the people who care about you the most—your parents. After all, no one else is likely to love you more or care as much about your well-being. Unfortunately, parents are often the last people to find out that their child may have a drug problem.

Why is this so? If you're a child or teen with a drug problem, you may feel embarrassed or ashamed to be involved in something that you know is illegal or harmful to you. Maybe you fear that your parents will punish or lecture you rather than help you find ways to stop using drugs. Or maybe your relationship with your family is part of your problem. Perhaps your parents don't get along well, don't support you, or abuse alcohol and other drugs themselves.

Of course, if your parents drink too much or use other drugs, they need to be aware that you may copy their behavior. They'll need to stay drug-free if they want you to do so. Parents can be the strongest influence in keeping their kids off drugs. A recent study published in the *Journal of the American Medical Association* found that teens who feel close to their parents are more likely to stay away from drugs.

What if you can't turn to your parents? Many kids find that confiding in another family member—an older brother or sister, a grandparent, or an aunt or uncle whom they feel close to—is the next best thing. You might also try talking to a favorite teacher or your school's counselor, psychologist, doctor, or nurse. These professionals are often trained to deal with drug abuse problems. Other people who may be able to help are scout leaders, sports coaches, or religious leaders. Remember, though, that no one can help you unless you first admit that you need help. This first step on the path to recovery is often the most difficult one.

Help Through Hotlines

Another way to find help or information about drug abuse is to check the yellow pages of your local phone book for listings like "Addiction," "Crisis Intervention,"

As his daughter grasps his finger, a former drug user in Miami, Florida, receives applause for completing a court-ordered drug treatment program. On the right behind him, Barry McCaffrey, the director of the federal government's Office of National Drug Control Policy, looks on.

"Drugs," or "Self-Help Groups." There you'll find phone numbers for local, county, state, and national drug abuse and prevention hotlines.

A hotline is usually a toll-free phone number that you can call 24 hours a day for help with a problem. Operators are often volunteers who are trained to listen to what you have to say and not judge you. You won't have to identify yourself if you don't want to, and your discussion remains confidential. No one else has to know about your phone call.

Hotline counselors can also tell you who to contact

in your area. In the back of this book, you will also find a list of some of the most well-known national drug abuse treatment and prevention organizations. Many of these groups have local chapters across the country.

Drug Abuse Treatment Programs

In some ways, treating drug addiction is more difficult than treating drug overdoses. This is because there is no "miracle cure" for drug addiction. Even after an alcoholic has stopped drinking and undergone treatment to stay sober, for example, he or she remains a "recovering alcoholic." This means that drinking alcohol again even once can put that person back on the road to addiction.

Being addicted or dependent on drugs is not necessarily a death sentence, however. Drug addiction is a treatable disease, and a wide variety of programs is available to help people become and stay drug-free.

Outpatient Treatment

This kind of program requires patients to attend scheduled therapy sessions, but patients are free to return home after each treatment. One of the features of outpatient counseling is education about what drugs can do to you and what "addiction" means. One type of **outpatient treatment** program provides a structured plan of individual, group, and family counseling. The patient usually attends sessions once a week for up to a couple of years. This kind of program is especially useful for youngsters in an early stage of addiction, or for those who are at low risk of relapsing (returning to drug abusing).

Another type of outpatient treatment is a one-day program of intense counseling. This works best for former drug abusers who are not at great risk for relapsing and are able to live at home. Such programs usually last from early morning until late afternoon.

Inpatient Treatment

When drug problems are severe or a patient is likely to relapse, **inpatient treatment** may be necessary. In these highly structured programs, patients stay in a hospital-like facility and are restricted from outside influences. They must participate in intensive counseling and treatment over several weeks or months. A medical staff is usually on hand in case patients experience severe or life-threatening withdrawal symptoms.

Residential Treatment

Drug abusers who have tried other types of treatment with little or no success and who are at great risk of relapsing are usually entered in a residential treatment program. This is a supervised, round-the-clock program during which patients live at a center for up to a year or more. They are carefully supervised by trained counselors, mental health workers, and medical doctors. The main goal of such treatment programs is not only to help addicts recover physically, but also to help them develop the skills to change their lives and avoid drugs for good.

Some patients of residential treatment centers "graduate" to halfway houses: home-away-from-home

Drug abusers with severe problems and those who have been unsuccessful at other types of treatment usually benefit from a residential treatment program, such as this one in California.

residences where recovering addicts live together for further support before going out on their own. Although they are supervised, residents of halfway houses usually begin to return to work and gradually reenter the "outside world." Once recovering addicts have proved that they can return to the stresses of everyday life without relapsing, they are ready to move back home.

Treating Drug Addiction with Drugs

For addictions to certain drugs, a recovery program might also involve taking another drug that helps the addict avoid painful and sometimes dangerous with-drawal symptoms. For example, the treatment of a heroin addiction usually includes administering a milder drug called **methadone**, an opiate-like drug that is not as addictive as morphine and heroin. Although methadone can cause dependence, its effects are longer-lasting but less intense than those of heroin. This is why it is viewed as an effective way to treat longtime heroin addicts whose bodies have adapted to require a constant supply of opiates.

Patients undergoing methadone treatment must appear at their treatment clinic each day for a single dose of methadone. They are also tested for the presence of other drugs in their bodies. If they are "clean" (have taken no other drugs), they are given their methadone tablet, which they must take in the presence of a worker at the center.

As recovering heroin addicts show they can be trusted, they are permitted to come to the clinic less frequently and take home their supply of methadone, which they continue to take daily. With this type of treatment, heroin dependence can usually end in one to three weeks.

Acute-Care Hospital Treatment

The most intensive level of drug treatment takes place within acute-care hospital programs (in this case, "acute" means "very serious" or "critical"). These programs are often located in major medical centers and are staffed by highly trained psychiatrists, psychologists,

These people are attempting to break the powerful hold that alcohol has on their lives by attending an Alcoholics Anonymous (AA) meeting. AA is the most widely known self-help group in the world. Members are recovering alcoholics who offer ongoing support for one another.

medical doctors, social workers, specially trained nurses, addiction counselors, and occupational therapists.

A typical stay in an acute-care program is brief—from 3 to 30 days—but often very expensive because of the number of trained medical personnel on hand. Acute-care programs aim to provide a number of services to patients with drug addictions. First, staff members immediately conduct a range of tests to determine the patient's physical and mental condition. Next, they stabilize the patient and provide a safe method of withdrawal from the addictive substance. After these steps are completed, they help the patient realize how severe his or her problem is and provide education about the nature of drug addiction. Finally, they strongly encourage the patient to seek other levels of treatment (such as a residential program).

Self-Help Groups

Recovering addicts often benefit from ongoing support for their drug problems. Self-help programs are usually free, drop-in meetings catered to specific addictions. Participants listen to others speak about their alcohol or other drug addictions. In this way, each person gives and receives support.

The most popular self-help group in the United States is Alcoholics Anonymous (AA). Today, AA has nearly 2 million members around the world. AA treatment is built on what is called the Twelve Steps Program. Members admit that the drug has ruined their lives and that they are responsible for stopping their alcohol consumption. Although AA is not a religious organization, members also acknowledge that a "higher power"—a positive force greater than themselves—can help them recover. AA members must also try to make amends for any wrong or harm they may have done to others while under the influence of alcohol.

One of the principles of AA and other self-help organizations, such as Narcotics Anonymous, Cocaine Anonymous, and Drugs Anonymous, is that recovering addicts help one another by sharing their experiences in regular meetings. Usually, longtime members also "sponsor" newer members by agreeing to be available outside meetings should recovering addicts need help.

For Families and Friends of Drug Abusers

Offshoots of self-help programs, such as Al-Anon, Adult Children of Alcoholics (ACOA), and Narc-Anon, cater specifically to families and friends of recovering addicts. These organizations help members rebuild relationships that drug addiction has torn apart.

The programs teach members how to avoid behaving in a way that protects the addict from the consequences of his or her abuse. For example, one should not call in sick on behalf of an addict who cannot make it to work, or help the person get out of jail if he or she has been arrested for drug use. These programs also teach family and friends that you cannot force an addict to seek help. The decision to get help and stop abusing drugs ultimately rests with the addict.

When a family member or friend has a serious alcohol or other drug problem, another approach is a process called intervention. In an intervention, the drug abuser is confronted in a constructive and nonthreatening way by professionals trained in drug treatment or by those who care about the abuser. Successful interventions take place when the abuser is not intoxicated or experiencing withdrawal symptoms. Those who are confronting the abuser need to acknowledge that they cannot make the abuser do something he or she is not ready to do. They must also name very specific examples—dates, times, and events—showing how drugs are causing harm. And if the abuser seems ready to seek help, they must be ready with appropriate information—the address and phone number of a drug treatment center, for example.

Admitting to a drug problem is a big step, and it can be frightening. That's why it's important to remember that if a drug abuser denies the problem or refuses help, you should always look for another opportunity to bring up the subject. The next time, you may get the person you care about to realize that he or she needs help.

Staying Drug-Free

Recovering from alcohol or other drug addictions is a lifelong process. It involves changing one's behavior, attitudes, and way of seeing oneself and one's life. It means giving up not only drinking or using other drugs, but also the whole way of life that comes with it.

The best drug treatment program for each person depends on many factors, including the individual's personality, social situation, age, family circumstances, and degree and length of addiction or dependence. No treatment can guarantee a cure, but all treatments offer hope to people who feel as though drugs have taken over their lives.

As you now know, your best bet for keeping your life on track is *never to start using drugs*. Plenty of programs in schools, community centers, and even in the media (TV, radio, newspapers, magazines, books, and the Internet) can help you learn how to avoid drugs. In Chapter 5, we'll examine some of these prevention programs.

Teenagers decorate their school gym for an anti-drug rally. Does your school sponsor drug prevention events like this? If not, maybe you and your friends can create one.

PREVENTING DRUG ABUSE

How do you stop people from abusing drugs in the first place? That's a good question, and one with many answers. Let's take a look at some of them.

Drugs and the Law

For decades, the U.S. government has attempted to control drug abuse by passing laws that make using certain dangerous drugs illegal. These laws also make it against the law to possess or sell such substances.

Each year, the federal government spends millions of dollars trying to keep illegal drugs out of the United States. At the nation's borders, police with drug-sniffing dogs check cars, boats, and travelers' baggage in an effort to stem the tide of drugs being smuggled into the country. Every state has a similar agency that aims to keep illegal drugs out of its own region. And in cities and towns

At a pier in Brooklyn, New York, U.S. Customs agents load eight tons of marijuana, with a street value of $19 million, onto a truck. The shipment was seized from nine members of a Colombian drug organization.

across America, local police fight to prevent street sales and abuse of illegal drugs.

The federal government has cracked down on legal drug use as well. Some laws regulate how and where alcohol and cigarette advertising can appear. One of the most recent laws, which went into effect in April 1999, bans cigarette advertising on billboards. In 1997 and 1998, several states sued the country's biggest tobacco companies in an attempt to recover billions of dollars spent on medical care for those who suffered health problems resulting from years of tobacco use.

Drugs and Education

In 1998, President Clinton instituted a $2 billion, five-year drug education campaign that includes a series of advertisements in newspapers and on radio and TV. The program is aimed at children, in the hope of convincing them to stay away from drugs

Since 1987, public schools have been required by the federal government to teach drug prevention. Some school- and community-based drug education programs are supported by government funds.

As a result of such programs, more kids and adults today are aware of the hazards of drug use than at any other time in U.S. history. Although knowing what drugs can do to you is an important first step to staying drug-free, it is also important to know how to avoid situations where drugs are available, and especially important to learn how to say no to harmful drugs.

Saying No and Meaning It

The desire to fit in with the crowd can be a very powerful feeling. But there are ways to avoid using drugs while still feeling like part of the gang. If you want to do what's best for you, you have to stand up for yourself.

This isn't always easy. It takes courage. But if you do say no to drugs, you may find that other friends who may have been afraid to speak up will take your side, because they'll know they are not alone.

In D.A.R.E.—the Drug Abuse Resistance Education program—law officers visit schools to inform kids and their parents about the dangers of drug use. The D.A.R.E. police car shown here is a Corvette that was confiscated from an arrested drug dealer.

Here are some tips on how to refuse drugs and mean it:

- Be aware. Knowing what drugs can do to you will make it easier to resist them.
- Be prepared. Find out in advance when and where you might end up in a situation where others are doing drugs—say, at a party. Then decide whether you really want to be there. If you do, be sure that you can say no to alcohol or other drugs.

- Be decisive. Make your "no, thanks" be the end of the discussion.
- Be busy. Have some places you have to be—an after-school club or practice, a friend's house, a job, or your own home.
- Be smart. Anyone who pressures you to take drugs is not your friend. Stay away from people who urge you to try drugs or who offer them to you.

Some kids have also found that getting involved in drug-free activities such as dances, movies, or community service projects helps them avoid drugs. Others have found that organizing their own drug awareness program for their school, church, or community not only helps them stay "clean," but also encourages others to do the same.

Using Your Head

After you say no a few times to cigarettes, alcohol, marijuana, or other drugs, you'll find it easier to turn down anything you don't want. It doesn't take a lot of brains to start using drugs. Why not *use* your mind instead of losing it to drugs? Don't be afraid to ask for help if you need it. Everyone—no matter what age you are—can use help now and then. Your real friends—the people who truly love you—will help you say no to using drugs, and say yes to using your head.

GLOSSARY

addiction—a condition of some drug users that is caused by repeated drug use. An addicted user becomes physically dependent on the drug and continues to take it, despite severe negative consequences. Obtaining and using the drug take over the person's life.

aerosol—a substance made of tiny liquid or solid particles suspended in a gas.

amphetamine—an addictive stimulant, or a class of stimulants that includes this chemical.

binge drinking—uncontrolled or excessive indulgence in alcohol, especially in a brief period of time.

cocaine—a powerful stimulant made from the leaves of the coca plant and usually sold as a white powder. Cocaine is highly addictive.

crack—an extremely addictive, solid form of cocaine made by mixing the drug with other substances and then heating and hardening it.

Ecstasy—the chemical MDMA (3,4-methylenedioxymethamphetamine); a combination of a hallucinogen called MDA and the stimulant methamphetamine.

gateway drug—a relatively weak drug whose use may lead to experimentation with stronger drugs like cocaine and heroin. Alcohol, nicotine, and marijuana are considered gateway drugs.

hallucinogen—a substance that distorts the user's perception of objects or events, or causes the user to perceive objects or visions that are not real.

heroin—a drug made from the milky juice of the poppy plant called *Papaver somniferum*. Heroin is the common name given to diacetylmorphine, one of the strongest of the opiate drugs. It is highly addictive. Some street names for heroin are: "H," "horse," "smack," "junk," and "black tar."

inhalant—any common but toxic chemical that is inhaled through the nose or mouth to cause intoxication. Many household products, such as correction fluid, felt-tip markers, model airplane glue, and nail polish remover, are abused as inhalants.

inpatient treatment—a highly structured drug rehabilitation program in which a person stays at, or is checked into, the clinic or hospital where the treatment will take place. Inpatient treatment is also called residential treatment.

LSD—the chemical called lysergic acid diethylamide, a hallucinogenic (mind-altering) drug made from a fungus that grows on the rye plant.

marijuana—a psychoactive drug derived from the *Cannabis sativa* plant that is smoked or eaten for its initial effect of euphoria or relaxation.

methadone—an opioid, or synthetic drug devised to produce effects similar to opiates, which was developed during World War II as a less addictive substitute for morphine. Methadone produces less intense but longer-lasting effects than heroin or morphine. It is commonly used to treat addiction to the two drugs.

methamphetamine—a powerful form of amphetamine that is legally available by prescription under the name Desoxyn but is also illegally manufactured in different forms under various names, including "crank" and "ice."

nicotine—the highly addictive substance found in the tobacco plant and in all tobacco products.

opium—a drug derived from the milky juice of the poppy plant *Papaver somniferum.*

outpatient treatment—a drug rehabilitation program in which a person lives at home and attends scheduled therapy and education sessions.

overdose—too large a dose, as of a medicine or drug. Depending on the substance, an overdose can cause coma, organ failure, or death.

paranoia—extreme, irrational distrust of others, accompanied by exaggerated fears.

peer pressure—words or actions by a friend, a sibling, or someone else of your own age group that make you feel as though you have to follow their behavior to fit in.

physical dependence—a state in which a drug user's body chemistry has adapted to require regular doses of the drug to function normally. Stopping the drug causes withdrawal symptoms.

predisposed—having a tendency toward a particular action or thing. Some people are predisposed to develop drug addictions.

psychoactive—affecting the mind or behavior.

psychological dependence—the state of addiction in which certain brain changes create strong cravings to use a drug, even if the user has no withdrawal symptoms or physical urge to do so.

solvent—a liquid, such as water, alcohol, or ether, that can dissolve another substance to form a solution.

stimulant—a drug that increases the body's activities, including heart rate and blood pressure.

tolerance—a condition in which a drug user needs to increase the dosage of the drug in order to reach the same level of high that was previously achieved by using smaller amounts.

withdrawal—a process that occurs when a person who is physically dependent on a drug stops taking the drug.

BIBLIOGRAPHY

Center for Substance Abuse Prevention (CSAP). "Tips for Teens About Alcohol." National Clearinghouse for Alcohol and Drug Information (NCADI) Publication #PHD323. Rockville, MD: CSAP, 1996.

_____. "Tips for Teens About Crack and Cocaine." NCADI Publication #PHD640. Rockville, MD: CSAP, 1996.

_____. "Tips for Teens About Hallucinogens." NCADI Publication #PHD642. Rockville, MD: CSAP, 1996.

_____. "Tips for Teens About Marijuana." NCADI Publication #PHD641. Rockville, MD: CSAP, 1996.

Harvard School of Public Health. "A Guide for Teens: Does Your Friend Have an Alcohol or Other Drug Problem? What You Can Do to Help." NCADI Publication #PHD688. Boston: Harvard School of Public Health, 1994.

McFarland, Rhoda. *Drugs and Your Parents*. New York: Rosen Publishing Group, 1997.

Mothers Against Drunk Driving (MADD). "The Unbelievable Truth About Being a Teenage Boy." http://www.madd.org/UNDER21/youth_guys.shtml. Irving, TX: MADD, 1998.

_____. "The Unbelievable Truth About Being a Teenage Girl." http://www.madd.org/UNDER21/youth_girls.shtml. Irving, TX: MADD, 1998.

National Institute on Drug Abuse (NIDA). "How Not to Get High, Get Stupid, Get AIDS: A Guide to Partying." NCADI Publication #PHD622. Bethesda, MD: NIDA, 1993.

Trapani, Margi. *Inside a Support Group: Help for Teenage Children of Alcoholics*. New York: Rosen Publishing Group, 1997.

FIND OUT MORE ABOUT GETTING HELP FOR DRUG ABUSE

The following list includes agencies, organizations, and websites that provide information about drugs of abuse and where to go for help with a drug problem.

Many national organizations have local chapters listed in your phone directory. Look under "Drug Abuse and Addiction" to find resources in your area.

Agencies and Organizations in the United States

Al-Anon Family Group Headquarters
1600 Corporate Landing Parkway
Virginia Beach, VA 23454-5617
http://www.al-anon.alateen.org
757-563-1600
800-344-2666 (United States)
800-443-4525 (Canada)

Alateen
P.O. Box 862
Midtown Station
New York, NY 10018
212-302-7240
800-344-2666

Alcoholics Anonymous (AA) World Services
475 Riverside Drive, 11th Floor
New York, NY 10115
212-870-3400
http://www.alcoholics-anonymous.org

American Council for Drug Education
164 West 74th Street
New York, NY 10023
212-758-8060
800-488-DRUG (3784)
http://www.acde.org/
wlittlefield@phoenixhouse.org

Center for Substance Abuse Treatment
Information and Treatment Referral Hotline
11426-28 Rockville Pike, Suite 410
Rockville, MD 20852
800-662-HELP (4357)

Children of Alcoholics Foundation, Inc.
555 Madison Avenue, 4th Floor
New York, NY 10022
212-754-0656
800-359-COAF (2623)

Cocaine Anonymous
6125 Washington Boulevard, Suite 202
Culver City, CA 90232
800-347-8998

Cocaine Hotline
800-COCAINE (262-2463)

Drugs Anonymous
P.O. Box 473
Ansonia Station, NY 10023
212-874-0700

Just Say No International
2000 Franklin Street, Suite 400
Oakland, CA 94612
800-258-2766

**Mothers Against
    Drunk Driving (MADD)**
P.O. Box 541688
Dallas, TX 75354-1688
http://www.madd.org

Narcotics Anonymous (NA)
P.O. Box 9999
Van Nuys, CA 91409
818-773-9999

**National Adolescent
    Suicide Hotline**
800-621-4000

**National Center on Addiction
    and Substance Abuse at
    Columbia University**
152 West 57th Street, 12th Floor
New York, NY 10019-3310
212-841-5200 or 212-956-8020
http://www.casacolumbia.org/home.htm

**National Clearinghouse
    for Alcohol and Drug
    Information (NCADI)**
P.O. Box 2345
Rockville, MD 20847-2345
800-729-6686
800-487-4889 TDD
800-HI-WALLY (449-2559, Children's Line)
http://www.health.org/

**Office of National
    Drug Control Policy**
750 17th Street, N.W., 8th Floor
Washington, DC 20503
888-395-NDCP (6327)
http://www.whitehousedrugpolicy.gov/
ondcp@ncjrs.org

**Parents' Resource Institute
    for Education (PRIDE)**
3610 DeKalb Technology Parkway,
Suite 105
Atlanta, GA 30340
770-458-9900
http://www.prideusa.org/

Shalom, Inc.
311 South Juniper Street,
Room 900
Philadelphia, PA 19107
215-546-3470

**Students Against Driving
    Drunk (SADD)**
P.O. Box 800
Marlboro, MA 01750
508-481-3568

Agencies and Organizations in Canada

**Addictions Foundation
  of Manitoba**
1031 Portage Avenue
Winnipeg, Manitoba R3G 0R8
204-944-6277
http://www.mbnet.mb.ca/crm/health/afm.html

**Addiction Research
  Foundation (ARF)**
33 Russell Street
Toronto, Ontario M5S 2S1
416-595-6100
800-463-6273 in Ontario

**Alberta Alcohol and
  Drug Abuse Commission**
10909 Jasper Avenue, 6th Floor
Edmonton, Alberta T5J 3M9
http://www.gov.ab.ca/aadac/
800-663-1880 in British Columbia

**British Columbia Prevention
  Resource Center**
96 East Broadway, Suite 211
Vancouver, British Columbia V5T 1V6
604-874-8452
800-663-1880 in British Columbia

**Canadian Centre
  on Substance Abuse**
75 Albert Street, Suite 300
Ottawa, Ontario K1P 5E7
613-235-4048
http://www.ccsa.ca/

**Ontario Healthy Communities
  Central Office**
180 Dundas Street West, Suite 1900
Toronto, Ontario M5G 1Z8
416-408-4841
http://www.opc.on.ca/ohcc/

Websites

**D.A.R.E. (Drug Abuse
  Resistance Education)
  for Kids**
http://www.dare-america.com/index2.htm

Join Together Online
http://www.jointogether.org/sa/

**National Institute
  on Drug Abuse (NIDA)**
http://www.nida.nih.gov

**Partnership for a
  Drug-Free America**
http://www.drugfreeamerica.org/

Reality Check
http://www.health.org/reality/

**U.S. Department of
  Education Safe and
  Drug-Free Schools Program**
http://inet.ed.gov/offices/OESE/SDFS

D espite what you may have heard, selling illegal drugs will not make you rich. In 1998, two professors, Steven Levitt from the University of Chicago and Sudhir Venkatesh from Harvard University, released a study of how drug gangs make and distribute money. To get accurate information, Venkatesh actually lived with a drug gang in a midwestern city.

You may be surprised to find out that the average street dealer makes just about $3 an hour. You'd make more money working at McDonald's! Still think drug-dealing is a cool way to make money? What other after-school jobs carry the risk of going to prison or dying in the street from a gunshot wound?

Drug-dealing is illegal, and it kills people. If you're thinking of selling drugs or you know someone who is, ask yourself this question: is $3 an hour worth dying for or being imprisoned?

WHAT A DRUG GANG MAKES IN A MONTH*

	During a Gang War	No Gang War
INCOME (money coming in)	$ 44,500	$ 58,900
Other income (including dues and blackmail money)	10,000	18,000
TOTAL INCOME	**$ 54,500**	**$ 76,900**
EXPENSES (money paid out)		
Cost of drugs sold	$ 11,300	$ 12,800
Wages for officers and street pushers	25,600	37,600
Weapons	3,000	1,600
Tributes (fees) paid to central gang	5,800	5,900
Funeral and other expenses	10,300	4,200
TOTAL EXPENSES	**$ 56,000**	**$ 62,100**
TOTAL INCOME	$ 54,000	$ 76,900
MINUS TOTAL EXPENSES	- 56,000	- 62,100
TOTAL AMOUNT OF PROFIT IN ONE MONTH	**- 1,500**	**14,800**

* adapted from "Greedy Bosses," *Forbes*, August 24, 1998, p. 53. Source: Levitt and Venkatesh.

INDEX

PICTURE CREDITS

RICHARD KOZAR has authored several books for Chelsea House, including *Hillary Rodham Clinton*, *Infamous Pirates*, and *Inventors and Their Discoveries*. He lives in western Pennsylvania with his wife, Heidi, and daughters Caty and Macy.

BARRY R. McCAFFREY is director of the Office of National Drug Control Policy (ONDCP) at the White House and a member of President Bill Clinton's cabinet. Before taking this job, General McCaffrey was an officer in the U.S. Army. He led the famous "left hook" maneuver of Operation Desert Storm that helped the United States win the Persian Gulf War.

STEVEN L. JAFFE, M.D., received his psychiatry training at Harvard University and the Massachusetts Mental Health Center and his child psychiatry training at Emory University. He has been editor of the *Newsletter of the American Academy of Child and Adolescent Psychiatry* and chairman of the Continuing Education Committee of the Georgia Psychiatric Physicians' Association. Dr. Jaffe is professor of child and adolescent psychiatry at Emory University. He is also clinical professor of psychiatry at Morehouse School of Medicine, and the director of Adolescent Substance Abuse Programs at Charter Peachford Hospital in Atlanta, Georgia.